# THE Sensual Feminine Life

By Jen Bugajsky

*The Good Girl*

To contact the author: www.TheFreedomKeys.com





Book design by Rachel Valliere of Printed Page Studios.

ISBN: 979-8-9861917-0-6

# AWARENESS & DISCOVERY

*Understanding the societal, cultural and religious views that have held you back from your sexual freedom*

# INTRODUCTION TO THE

## Layout for Each Key

### Theme of the Key

- Explanation of the key for that week
- What you will learn in each key for that week

### Your Role

- Explanation of your role within the key for that week
- Goals

### Topics

- From religion to societal influences, each week of each key will have a range of topics for you to think about in relation to the key.

### Witnessing

- I encourage you to go at your own pace. We all have an internal desire for love and approval; however, it can feel vulnerable to look inside yourself and share with another sister the most intimate thoughts and parts of you.
- I have created a safe space where I, Jen, sit in my vulnerability and give women permission to be raw and real. Trust me when I share with you that I have been on this journey. Some stories from other women may be referenced in this section as well. Rest assured I have received their approval to share their stories with you, and some of the names have been changed to protect their identities (referenced with an *).
- Whether you are being witnessed and being seen for who you are, or you are witnessing another sister in her truth, it is a critical part of the journey.
- By sharing our stories, we unlock the closed doors and open ourselves to endless possibilities. These possibilities include experiencing real pleasure, satisfaction, and fulfillment in our lives. Together, we realize we are not alone in our feelings of guilt, shame, and fear in the face of previously forbidden pleasure.

### Exercises

- Each week of each key will close with some exercises. The more exercises you complete, the more value you will receive from the course. These exercises help you think in different ways and help open your mind to a variety of possibilities.

The Syllabus for subsequent weeks:

- Topics
- Witnessing
- Exercises

## Six Stages of Connecting with Our Body and Our Femininity

When it comes to getting to know our bodies, there are six phases of growth and evolution. Each one of us moves through these stages at various times in our lives. There is no right or wrong time. There is the time that is comfortable for us. There is also no right pace. Some women move through each stage at slower paces and some more quickly.

Regardless of where you are, you are exactly where you are meant to be. There is no race to the finish line. In fact, you will learn to know yourself better as you spend time within each of the phases. Some women may never get past a certain stage. If they don't, that is okay because that is what is meant for their journey in this lifetime.

### KEY 1: Awareness & Discovery

The first Key is awareness. We can't change what we are not aware of. Once we are aware of ideas and concepts that trigger us, we can learn how to train ourselves to respond in a better way. Awareness can be scary or exciting since it is the first step in the journey. It's important to not do too much in this Key. Awareness can be overwhelming and it's okay to just sit with the feelings for a time.

#### In This Key

You will be cracked wide open to the naked truth around your sexuality as a woman, how your sexual energy is the creative force within you, and how embracing your sexual energy is the key to success in life and relationships. You will learn it is not your fault and how historic conditioning has molded your perspective on sex, love, and relationships. You will learn to take inspired action to break free from this conditioning and step into the radiant, sexual, beautiful goddess of a woman you were created to be.

#### Your Role: Good Girl

A good girl is reserved, maybe even repulsed by the subject of sex. She is somewhat closed off to her sexuality. She may not have time for sexual connection and doesn't find it important to her success and happiness. This is a place where we all begin to understand the naked truth about sex, love, and relationships.

### Key 2: Permission to Be Curious

The second Key and next principle is Curiosity. If you want to dive into your own pleasure and experience more fulfillment in your sexual experiences and in life, you must be curious. Curiosity is a desire or eagerness to learn more. A woman who is in her feminine energy and power asks questions and is willing to explore outside of her comfort zone.

### Key 3: Acceptance and Personal Responsibility

The third Key is acceptance and taking personal responsibility. You give yourself permission to the possibilities of knowing, loving, and honoring this beautiful sexy, gorgeous, elegant body you have been gifted. This is a time of healing and loving your body for you. No one can take care of your body better than you. When you learn to love and accept your body, you allow yourself to experience the pleasures your body can provide.

### Key 4: Playing with Your Feminine Energy

The fourth Key is where the fun really begins. You have been given a permission slip to enjoy your own pleasure. When you allow yourself to own your own pleasure, you can begin to have fun and enjoy your sexuality as a woman. You allow yourself to explore and really start enjoying the sensations your body is feeling. Some of it might be new, and that is okay because our bodies were made to experience pleasure.

### Key 5: Trust, Polarity, and Surrender

The fifth Key is learning to let go of control. It feels good to have certainty and a plan because that is how you have been taught to get things done. However, if you truly want to experience intimacy with your partner through a deeper connection or a more orgasmic sexual experience, you must learn to trust and surrender to your God-given, feminine nature.

### Key 6: Worthy and Deserving

The sixth Key and principle moving through this stage is your presence and owning your value as a woman. Presence is the physical, emotional, and energetic way you show up as who you are. You are "tuned in" and comfortable expressing your true thoughts, feelings, values, and potential. When a woman has presence, she owns her value and shows up confident about who she is and the choices she makes.

for Key 1

# HISTORIC CONDITIONING AROUND BEING A WOMAN

## THEME: *Awareness & Discovery*

The first Key is awareness. We must be aware of a problem before change can begin. Some women might not want to go here because they don't want to talk about it or they believe sexuality is not important.

In this section, we will address some key components regarding what is getting in the way of us loving our bodies and embracing our sexuality as women. The raw, real, and naked truth is that sexuality and the way we have been taught to think about sex and our bodies is at the core of our body shaming.

## YOUR ROLE: *The Good Girl*

A good girl is reserved, maybe even repulsed, by the subject of sex. She is somewhat closed off to her sexuality. She follows the rules. She does what she is told. She strives for perfection. She may not have time for sexual connection and doesn't find it important to her success and happiness. She is someone who has lived by the constraints of the dogmatic system. She may even be disgusted by certain words used around sexuality.

She isn't interested in talking about sex. It might be painful. She might have never experienced real pleasure from sex and doesn't make it a priority. She might just do it with her husband because she feels obligated but doesn't always enjoy it. She also could be the person who has no interest in sex at all. This is the place where we all begin to understand the naked truth about sex, love, and relationships.

In this Key, you will be cracked wide open to the naked truth around your sexuality as a woman, how your sexual energy is the creative force within you, and how embracing this life force energy is the key to success in life and relationships. You will learn it is not your fault. You will learn how historic conditioning has molded your perspective on sex, love, and relationships. You will learn to take inspired action to break free from this conditioning and step into the beautiful, sensual goddess you were created to be.

## YOUR GOALS

- Be aware and track what topics "trigger" you to feel different emotions and feelings—not necessarily just bad emotions but all emotions and feelings. Start with 3–5.
- Take notice of the cause of the emotion. For example, if you feel guilt, why?
- Create your own goals.

## TOPIC 1: Historic Conditioning: The Truth About Sex

Let us first review what we were taught about sex and our bodies. Women seem to have two choices: to do things the way men do them (and not do them well because we are *women*) or hide (e.g., from scrutiny, judgment, violence).

In the Western hemisphere, we live in a patriarchal society where the focus has been on men and the masculine way of doing things. Women have had to work hard to get the same equality, opportunities, and rights as men (and we *still* aren't really "equal"). During this important development of history, we have lost a piece of our natural feminine nature along the way by trying to do things "like men" or do things in "masculine ways." To take things a step further, there is a key piece of our feminine nature that was never culturally passed down to us from generation to generation, so in fact we might never know it was missing.

With the desire to be strong, independent, and confident, many women have created a false presence. This lack of authenticity weakens their effectiveness, their self-esteem, and their ability to create more of what they desire in life. In essence, they are hiding behind the truth of themselves and who they are. That truth begins with owning their body and their sexuality as women. They may be strong and confident in many other aspects of their life, but when it comes to their body and their sexuality, they don't see it as important.

For thousands of years, women were never taught the beauty, benefits, and power that come with being a woman. We certainly were never taught to embrace our sexuality and our bodies. We have always struggled with truly loving, accepting, and treasuring our bodies for the beautiful, amazing creatures we are. We have been taught to protect ourselves from men, to hide, to not show up as "too sexy."

We need to reorganize our experiences as women so pleasure becomes a priority. When we suppress our erotic nature and our desires, we are allowing the patriarchy to take over and dull our radiance.

If you really want to have deep intimacy and connection with your partner or husband, you first must have a love affair with yourself. You must experience a deep intimacy and connection with yourself! You must make your pleasure a priority in your life. I am not talking about joy or a sense of peace. I am talking about physical pleasure. You have the birthright to experience pleasure in your life, and it is the key to what is holding you back from all you desire.

## TOPIC 2: What Were You Taught About Sex Growing Up?

After interviewing hundreds of men and women, these three responses were the most common answers to this very basic question.

1. Nothing; I didn't learn much about sex and my body.
2. I was told, "Don't do it before you are married."
3. Use protection.

Among the hundreds of people interviewed, there was only one woman who shared that she talked about sex with her kids. She happened to be Jewish. She shared that while she was growing up, she was asked all sorts of questions from her Christian friends who didn't have a clue about sex. She taught them things about sex and their bodies that they had never been told.

If you are someone who was raised in a faith and culture where sex, sexuality, and your body was not discussed, no wonder you have so many challenges in today's world. If we have no idea about the truth behind our bodies and our sexuality, how are we going to learn?

Talking to your kids about sex and their bodies is not the easiest topic; however, take some time to reflect on what you were taught—whether it was from your parents, school, religion, or culture—throughout your childhood and into your adult life.

How can we have a healthy society and teach future generations about sexuality when adults are not comfortable talking about sex and their bodies? It's okay to laugh and joke about farting, burping, peeing, and pooping. It's a little embarrassing, yet it still gets a good laugh. However, bring up the words sex, moaning, orgasm, masturbation, dirty talk, pleasure, cock, pussy... and listen to the room go silent.

As a culture, we need to stop suppressing our sexual desires and stop shaming the physical beauty of our bodies. I suggest that we encourage women to admit that we are sexual creatures with sexual desires. There is no need to be ashamed of our authentic nature. We are not "bad girls" if we think about our desires and our own pleasure. In fact, it makes us more powerful when we know our desires and what we want.

*The truth of who we are is hidden behind our perception of our bodies.*

The first step to creating a more satisfied and fulfilled sex life is to become aware of the conditioning we have around sexuality. Since sex has been a taboo subject, it is something that is not frequently discussed. Let's think about how we are supposed to embrace our true, natural sexuality of being a woman even though no one taught us what it really meant.

## TOPIC 3: Witnessing

Let me tell you, I was in this phase for a long time. I was scared because of my past. I had been sexually abused as a little girl by my grandfather and was confused about love, boys, and relationships.

At 16, I dated a guy who I previously had sex with, but, one day, even though I said "no" multiple times, I didn't have the courage to fight him off, and I ended up pregnant. As an adult, I was not interested in sex. It was not important to me. My ex-husband was not interested in sex either, so it was never a point of contention for us. I was protected. I was safe. I didn't really know I was hiding, but I was. I was hiding behind the pain so I didn't have to face it. I could have stayed there and lived what I considered a comfortable life.

I also was repulsed by certain language used around sexuality. When I heard the word *pussy*, I cringed. Yikes! When I heard that women took mirrors and looked at themselves, I wanted to barf. When I heard that women drew and colored pictures of their vaginas, I thought they were absolutely crazy! Yes, I was a prude. I prided myself on being known as "the good Catholic girl."

What I loved about this phase of my journey was that the women and sisters around me loved me where I was. They never pushed me to go faster. They never told me I was wrong. They understood where I was coming from. They understood there were layers of deep pain that I wasn't even aware of that I needed to work through. They always encouraged me to continue to go deeper. It is because of my faith and belief in God that I was able to move through this phase to become more curious. I welcome you to this space and want you to know that whatever feelings come up for you are okay and completely normal.

## EXERCISE 1

Review the Freedom Keys Stages: Do you identify with "the good girl"? Check more than one, if applicable.

a. **What aspects of "the good girl" stand out for you?**

- ☐ Closed off to sex
- ☐ Reserved, conservative
- ☐ Repulsed by the thought or certain words/ phrases around sex
- ☐ Rule follower/people pleaser
- ☐ Striving for perfection—the desire to do it "right" or "perfect"

b. **What are your current thoughts and situation around sex? How do you feel about your answer?**

- ☐ I rarely think about it; I am not interested in having sex.
- ☐ I do it with my husband/partner, but I don't really enjoy it.
- ☐ I don't have time for sex; I am too busy.
- ☐ I used to enjoy sex, but I have lost my desire and libido.
- ☐ My partner wants it, but I am typically not interested.
- ☐ I want sex, but my partner is not interested.
- ☐ I do it with my partner, but not often. It takes a long time for me to enjoy myself.
- ☐ I like having sex and am curious but scared to try new things.
- ☐ I am ashamed of admitting I have sexual desires and fantasies.

c. **What feelings come up in your body when you think about your current sexual situation?**

- ☐ Sad
- ☐ Afraid/Scared/Fearful
- ☐ Mad/Angry/Frustrated
- ☐ Happy/Excited
- ☐ Alive/Turned on

## EXERCISE 2

**How do you feel about being witnessed?**

- ☐ I am a private person and don't like to share.
- ☐ I fear what others will think.
- ☐ I don't want other people knowing my business.
- ☐ I am uncomfortable with sharing, especially if I don't know the person.
- ☐ I am not sure what to share.
- ☐ I don't want people I know to know my stuff.
- ☐ I have no problem sharing with anyone.

**Noticing Homework:**

- Notice words or phrases you say all the time.
- Notice how your body feels.
- Notice if someone says something that triggers you.
- Notice if you get triggered by the exercises or the homework.

## EXERCISE 3

**Reflect on what you were taught about sex.**

- What did my parents or school teach me about sex?
- Have I ever felt shameful about my body and my sexuality?
- Did I feel comfortable talking with my parents about sex?
- Did I have someone I could talk to about sex?

Write down everything you believe about sex even if you know the beliefs are not true (i.e., the idea that "good girls don't do naughty things" may not be one you want to believe, but you still do).

Make two columns. Divide all your beliefs into these two categories. You can add to "What I want to believe" if more things come to you during the process.

Take the column with your internalized beliefs and write about how true or untrue these are for you. Where did they come from? Do you really believe this?

| *What I have internalized* | *What I want to believe* |
| --- | --- |
| | |

# Notes

# BOYS' VERSUS GIRLS' BODIES

## TOPIC 1: *Boys & Boners versus Girls & Their Period*

Now let me ask you another question. What were you taught about boys versus girls when it comes to our bodies and our genitals? These may or may not be true for you; however, when researching and interviewing many folks, these statements seemed to ring true for many. You may have other things you want to add, and that is okay, but the purpose of this section is awareness about the differences in what we teach boys and girls, specifically about their bodies.

| | |
|---|---|
| ◆ **Boys** have erections and ejaculation. | ◆ **Girls** have periods and need to protect themselves from pregnancy. |
| ◆ **Boys** love their penis. They take pride in how it looks and feels. | ◆ **Girls** think their genitals are disgusting; they don't even want to look at them. |
| ◆ **Boys** refer to their penis as "dick" or "cock" and proudly say it. | ◆ **Girls** don't know what to call their body part and are ashamed to talk about it. |
| ◆ **Boys** like to play with themselves. | ◆ **Girls** should not even consider playing with themselves. It is shameful, disgusting, and wrong. |

In society today, boys are taught to worship their penises. Women's genitals are not outside of our body, so we have a hard time seeing them.

Boys are taught from a young age that it feels good to explore their genitals, and girls are taught from a young age to not like their bodies. Boys feel powerful when they talk about their penis. Women are ashamed to talk about their vaginas, let alone connect with them. We live in a society that has shamed women and their bodies from a young age. No wonder we have so much unfulfillment in our lives. We are not embracing our sexuality, which is at the core of what defines us as women.

## TOPIC 2: Self-Pleasure and Masturbation

This is a topic that makes many people cringe. The label of masturbation has a negative connotation. Growing up, this was not a term used in discussion. It was saved for perverts who did not know how to handle their sexual energy and played with themselves to experience orgasm. It was a selfish act and was not something to consider. In fact, "playing with yourself" was considered "bad."

What were you taught about self-pleasure and masturbation? We know little boys play with themselves in the shower, but what are little girls taught about their bodies? Some women are afraid of the "M" word. Some women are relieved to hear someone else talking about it. Talking about it makes them feel not alone. Let me repeat that for the people in the back. You are not alone in your secret thoughts about self-pleasure.

Women are humans. We are creatures with animalistic needs and desires. There is nothing wrong with our needs and desires. In fact, when we suppress or starve them, that is the exact issue that causes us to disconnect with the fullest expression of ourselves. When I talk with women about this topic, some listen intently with a desire to learn, and others admit that they secretly explored their bodies but were ashamed. They, of course, didn't want to tell anyone about it. Regardless, they performed the act but still felt a sense of shame. Even though, physically, it felt good (and it should if you're doing it right!), it still felt wrong. They were bad. This is not something a "good girl" would do, Catholic or otherwise. They shouldn't focus on their own pleasure.

*A woman's feelings about her genitals and her body are directly related to how she experiences sex and her own pleasure. This has a ripple effect on how she truly connects with and experiences intimacy with her partner.*

## TOPIC 3: The Stages of the Female Lifecycle

There are three different stages in the female lifecycle: Maiden, Mother, and Crone; however the truth is that most of us were not taught to honor, celebrate, and embrace these phases of womanhood.

We were taught that, as young girls, you will hit a certain point in your life at which you will get your period. Once you reach this point in your life, you are now fertile and can have a baby. Your body will go through a lot of changes physically, emotionally, and hormonally. In addition, boys may find you more attractive and you need to be careful so you do not have unprotected sex and end up pregnant. Later in life, you will hit menopause. Your body will change, and your monthly cycle will be non-existent. Your body and hormones will never be the same.

What were you taught about the female body, your monthly cycle, and your role as a woman? When referring to a woman getting her period, did you experience a celebration? Or did you hear phrases like "It's that time of the month." "She is on the rag." "I have my monthly visitor." "Aunt Flo is here"?

There are many other derogatory terms that have been used for centuries concerning how to talk about a woman's body. For years we have been shaming the female body, especially during this time of the month. The implication is that it is gross and disgusting. As a result, we end up taking that same shame and relate that to our entire body and ourselves.

These three phases of the female lifecycle teach us how to live a balanced life, fully embody each phase of our lives, and celebrate with the waxing, waning, and fullness of the moon.

**The Maiden** energy is often depicted as the damsel in distress, but that is not truly who she is. The Maiden is independent and moves through the world with authenticity, intelligence, and a fierce curiosity. She is ready to leave home, enter the world, and go into the depths of self-discovery. The Maiden is associated with the waxing moon energy and represents the youthful chapters of a woman's life. When we are feeling unmotivated or overworked, the Maiden reminds us that we wake up each day to new beginnings and can start our day over anytime.

The Maiden personifies, joy, freedom, life, and every flourishing seed. She is a symbol and role model of what it means to fully embody your full self, light and shadow united. You can celebrate the inner Maiden anytime you are engaged in new beginnings, enthusiasm, or creativity. This is the beginning phase of womanhood.

**The Mother** is the natural caregiver and full of wisdom. She is fierce and full. She teaches us about standing on our own two feet. After we enter the world and come into womanhood, who are we? What have we learned as we step into our power? To what have we given birth? Giving birth does not necessarily mean physically giving birth to a baby. It also can be birthing in the sense of creating projects, dream partnerships, and businesses, too. The Mother is associated with the full moon energy and intentional rituals in life.

The Mother personifies manifestation, superabundance, and the kind of enduring love we should all know from our mothers and hold for ourselves and each other. This phase teaches us patience, understanding, and the incredible gifts of service. It is important to give yourself a little extra TLC just as you would for others. You feel your passion, fulfillment, and self-confidence rise when you celebrate your inner Mother and all that you birth into this world.

**The Crone** is known as the wise woman. She asks us to take a new perspective in life, to trust ourselves, and to let go of what we thought we knew as we move into a life that is more magical and intuitive. The wise woman knows the power of the shadows and the moon slipping away into the deep of the night sky. She knows the power of transmutation and is all knowing. The Crone is associated with the waning moon.

The Crone helps us ask hard questions so we move out of what is comfortable and known. She moves beyond the expectations and beliefs of society and steps into the fullness of who she was created to be. We celebrate our inner Crone anytime we embrace mystery, transformation, and release. To embrace your inner Crone is to truly let go. This does not mean death but rather the letting go of something that is no longer serving you.

## TOPIC 4: Witnessing

I remember one day I was talking with someone on the phone and one of my boys heard me say "self-pleasure." After I got off the phone, he squeamishly asked me if I was talking about "The M Word." I openly said yes and started a dialogue with him. We had never had a talk like this before. I vividly remember his energy. He was nervous but curious. He didn't say much, but I could feel his energy. I shared with him that self-exploration was normal, natural, and okay. He looked directly at me with this look of relief. This is a hard topic for adults to talk about amongst adults, let alone parent to child.

Another story comes to mind. I remember having the courage to ask a dear, trusted friend, who was always open and honest about life, if she ever masturbated as a kid. Her reply was, "Oh, yes, all the time. I used to play with my stuffed animals and use the water pressure in the shower." I remember feeling such relief that I was not alone. Granted, I didn't want to go shouting from the rooftops about my newfound knowledge, but what a relief to know I wasn't bad or wrong for exploring my body! I wasn't alone.

It is important for you to understand your cultural beliefs around experiencing pleasure before we can dive into the juiciness of experiencing all the beauty there is to it.

## EXERCISE 1

### Do the statements in Topic 1 feel true to you?

Are there any other generalizations about boys versus girls and their bodies that stick out to you? Write them down and share them with the group. You may think of a generalization that someone else hasn't thought of, but when you say it, they go, "Oh my goodness, yes that feels true!"

## EXERCISE 2

### How did you talk about your cycle and your period?

1. How old were you when you got your period?
2. What did your mom/grandma teach you about your period?
3. Was it a celebration, just another day, or a traumatic experience?
4. How did you talk about your period, and what did you call it?

## EXERCISE 3

### What were you taught about masturbation and self-pleasure?

1. Did my parents talk about self-pleasure or masturbation?
2. Did I experience self-pleasure as a child but never tell anyone?
3. Did I ever feel guilty or ashamed for enjoying my body?
4. Did I ever feel it was wrong to touch myself?

5. Did I ever feel guilty or ashamed for having sexual fantasies or desires?
6. Were I taught to sacrifice for others instead of experiencing pleasure for myself?
7. Do I feel pleasure is instant gratification and wrong?

## EXERCISE 4

**What were you taught about your body as a girl?**

1. What did you call your female body parts?
2. Did you feel comfortable talking about your breasts or your vagina?
3. Did you ever naturally explore your body, or did you feel it was wrong to touch yourself?
4. Did you learn that boys play with themselves for pleasure and little girls don't?

# Notes

# THE FORBIDDEN FRUIT

## TOPIC 1: Church and Societal Views: Good versus Bad

Women have a sexual nature at the core of who we are as humans. We need to learn how to teach women to embrace their erotic, natural, and wild sexuality rather than be afraid of it. We need to learn how to have a healthy and positive relationship with our bodies. So many of us probably were even taught different names for various body parts because there is shame around talking about them. Our bodies are a precious gift; however, we have never been taught how our power as a woman comes from our sexuality.

Instead, many rules have been created around our sexuality that are deemed "good" or "bad;" "right" or "wrong;" "evil" or "moral." Not everyone may agree with all of these, and, if that is the case, your parents must have been able to teach you a different perspective. However, millions of women suffer from beliefs that have been passed down from generation to generation that in fact are hurting us and we don't know it. If something is passed down through religion or through family, we typically don't question it. We take it on as a belief. Why would we think differently? Why would our parents teach us something that is core to the foundation of their being that we should question? Therein lies the problem. When it comes from the church and our family, we take it as the Word. Why would our parents teach us something that would harm us? Why would our parents teach us something that was wrong?

In the book *Red Hot and Holy: A Heretic's Love Story* by Sera Beak, she talks about her deep spiritual journey. She has a PhD in philosophy and has studied a variety of religions, and she was looking for the proof of who had "the right answer." What she realized was that there is no proof. You can't find the truth or the answer written anywhere. You must experience it! How many of us spend our lives trying to prove a point or prove someone else wrong? Or maybe we don't want to take a risk because we can't prove it is going to work for us?

We need to surrender the ego and the need to know and allow ourselves to feel what our heart is guiding us to do. This can be hard, especially when it comes to our faith, because for some people, the Bible is the way. If it's not written in the Bible, then it is wrong and should be challenged.

What did the church teach you about being a woman? What sort of role models do you have in your faith who are women? Only someone pure and pristine could be good enough to be the mother of God. Pressure from church society could cause thoughts, such as, "If you don't wait until marriage and save yourself, you are tainted and worn." and "You are not good enough."

Do you know how many women feel that they are not good enough? Many of us are not consciously saying this to ourselves; however, it is embedded subconsciously from years of generational teachings. If we are only taught to protect our virginity and not embrace our sexuality as a woman, what are we teaching women about being a woman? In general society, there are four boxes for women: the virgin, the whore, the mother, or the child. If you are not a mother, you are a child; if you are not a virgin, you must be a whore.

We don't have a good role model in the Christian Church that teaches how to embrace our sexuality. Mary Magdalene is the closest, and yet she has been portrayed as more provocative and someone we should not want to model ourselves after. Varying opinions about her exist; however, in 14 years of Catholic Church teachings, I personally was never taught that Mary Magdalene was a role model and woman I should follow. On the other hand, in Meggan Watterson's book, *Mary Magdalene Revealed*, we are told a story very different from the one with which most Christians are familiar. She explains why Mary Magdalene was portrayed as a prostitute and relates a more historical and theologically accurate depiction of who Mary was within the early Christian movement. Watterson states, "Mary's gospel says that we in fact are not sinful. We do not need to feel ashamed or unworthy for being human. In fact, our purpose is to be fully human. A true human being is one who is messy, a limited ego and a limitless soul. Her gospel, that was hidden, guides us to go inward so that we can see past the ego of our own lives to what is more real, and lasting, and infinite, and already here within."

It's like the people in power knew that a woman's power could be found in her sexuality, so they said, "Let's keep the power away from the women. Let's not tell them how to find their power. This way we can control them, and men can retain the power. If women believe that sex and pleasure are evil, taboo, or immoral, then they will not even think about tapping into that part of themselves. They won't have a clue what they are missing."

Women are either depriving themselves of feeling pleasure—believing that it is wrong, shameful, or selfish—or secretly sneaking around hiding the fact that they enjoy feeling pleasure. Either way, it's forbidden fruit. If I experience pleasure (or too much of it), I am "a bad girl," and if I deprive myself or sacrifice my own pleasures for others, I am "a good girl." We do not have to live in shame and guilt of past experiences that hold us back from embracing our sexuality.

## TOPIC 2: *Female Role Models and Sexuality*

Now that we have reflected a bit on some generalizations of what our culture and society have taught us about being "a good girl" versus "a bad girl," let's talk about direct role models we have had in our lives.

Role models are extremely important in our lives. Our parents are our first role models because they are our teachers. They intentionally teach us things they want us to learn, and we also learn things from them just by living with them. We learn what behaviors and actions we like or don't like. It is also important to remember that our parents can only teach or model what has been modeled for them. If your mother was not taught something, she obviously can't teach or model that for you. It is not her fault. It is what has been handed down from generation to generation until someone looks outside the box and learns something new.

If someone believes something is important, they will talk about it. You will know it is important to them. For example, take academics. Parents will talk to their kids about schoolwork and ensure they get good grades. It's top of mind. If your parents never talked about sexuality or showed you how to embrace your essence and sexuality as a woman, what are they modeling for you on this topic? They are modeling for you that sex and knowing what it means to be a woman is not important.

So many of us have a belief that sex is just not that important for women. We know it's important to men and they need it, but for women, it is more important to focus on being a good mom, wife, co-worker, church leader, friend, etc. No wonder we have a society of women who don't know how to embrace their sexuality. We have role models who ignore the topic (based on what they have been taught as well as society and church teachings that lead us to fear and shame regarding the concept of sex).

Do you secretly wish you had other female role models in your life to help influence and shape you into the woman you desire to become? My dad used to say that a teen needs at least 6–7 different role models of the same sex in their life to help them grow into the best version of themselves.

## TOPIC 3: Sacred Witnessing of Several Women

I was embarrassed that I had an abortion and premarital sex. I knew it was wrong in the eyes of the church, but at the time, I just couldn't make the decision to raise a child. I never sought counseling, and I have lived with this pain and shame for years. I felt so comfortable having a safe, sacred space to talk about the pain and guilt I had been holding onto for years. I felt that I had committed a sin and should be punished for the decisions I had made. This shame and guilt severely impacted my confidence and my ability to love myself.

Cheryl*, 45
Houston, TX

Many of my sexual beliefs were deeply rooted in my faith. I was taught to focus on pleasing the man first. As a result, I found myself in many abusive relationships where the man would use force and domination to instruct me to please him. I continued this pattern for several years and, in addition to pleasing him, I was not taught anything about my own pleasure. The focus was on me to please the man and not even think about what I could receive as a sexual act.

Janine*, 52
Juneau, AK

My husband and I rarely connect anymore inside or outside the bedroom. Yes, we have a nice family, but I feel we are living like roommates. The romance, passion, and connection have seemed to disappear. I remember when we used to enjoy being together, but now that we have kids, it's like my desire has faded and my body is no longer my own. I am so busy, I don't have the time to think about being intimate, let alone find the time to do it.

Mary*, 48
LaGuardia, NY

If I am being honest, I don't really enjoy sex. I do it with my husband because I know it is something that he wants and needs for his fulfillment. I was taught that it was my duty and obligation to please my husband. I want to make him happy, so I attend to his requests even when it doesn't feel good for me. Since sex is not something I have really enjoyed, I have never really thought about or focused on my own pleasure. It doesn't seem important to living a successful life, so I focus on being the good wife and partner to keep him satisfied.

Kelly*, 46
San Jose, CA

I have always been sexually active and enjoy being with my partner. While I do enjoy physical intimacy, I struggle with having vaginal orgasms. I feel like I am always in my head and can't really let myself surrender and let go to be fully immersed in the experience. I read about other women who enjoy the deep pleasures of intimacy, and yet I wonder if my body is just not made for it. Could I ever allow myself to fully surrender? Is it possible to really feel this kind of pleasure? Maybe I should just be happy with the experiences I have and not worry about making it better.

Lori*, 47
Greenbay WI

I am ashamed to admit, but when I hit 40, it was like something happened to my body. Suddenly, I had these sexual desires and fantasies show up. I found myself reading or listening to romance books or smutty novels, secretly wishing I was the woman in the book. I have this shame and guilt building up inside of me for even having these thoughts and desires. And it's not just the thoughts. When I read the juicy words in the book, I can feel the tingles in my body wishing it was me. Is there something wrong with me?

Sally*, 42
Orlando, FL

Do you relate to the thoughts and stories of any of these women? You are not alone in whatever thoughts and feelings you have around sex and the body. The truth is, society has created so much shame around sex that it makes it hard for women to talk about and become more educated on this topic. We need to create a safe place for women to feel comfortable sharing their own stories and listening to other women, so that, as a society, we can understand the truth about sex, love, and relationships and ultimately experience the deep levels of intimacy and connection we crave.

## TOPIC 4: *Sacred Witnessing Continued: My Sexual Experiences*

In my own journey, I was taught that sex was bad and evil. The sole purpose was for making babies. I was instructed not to have intercourse before marriage and that the act of intimacy was sacred and to be only performed within the sacrament of marriage. Any other use of my sexuality was a sin, and I would be condemned to hell if I participated in activities that were against God's word. The fear of God and being punished was instilled into my psyche. I was to stay away from sex and not embrace it. I was left with the belief that if I was sexually active for any other reason, I should be punished for not following the rules.

One of my very first boyfriends broke up with me after a year because I wouldn't have sex with him. I was devasted and couldn't eat or sleep for weeks. I couldn't understand why this would happen. I wasn't strong enough in my own beliefs of myself to stay strong in my decision and move on. I also had no one to talk with about it. I never told my mom why he broke up with me. So instead, I decided I wanted to get rid of this image of being known as "the good Catholic girl" and started exploring this taboo topic of sex. This event was a defining moment in my life and shaped my future experiences with men, sex, my thoughts about myself, and my own self-worth. I ended up having sex with a boy and became a bit promiscuous.

Here are a handful of thoughts I had about myself.

**I held onto the shame of having sex before I was married because**

- ... I am a bad girl for having sex outside of marriage.
- ... I am bad for having sex as a teenager.
- ... I am bad for having sex.
- ... I am bad for wanting to have sex.

**I held onto the guilt of**

- ... letting it happen—letting men use me for sex.
- ... having sex when it was a bad time of the month.
- ... allowing myself to get pregnant at 16.
- ... marrying a man to protect me and let me hide from who I really am.
- ... abusing my body because I didn't know how to love her.
- ... not respecting my body and giving her away to a man.
- ... not taking care of my body.
- ... not honoring, loving, and cherishing my body.
- ... ignoring my body like she didn't matter.
- ... not saying yes to my needs and my desires.

I had a really hard time coming out with my own story because I didn't want to chastise my faith. My parents would question me about my business, The Freedom Keys, and I would be somewhat reserved. I continued to poke holes in their faith, and it was very difficult to have a conversation with them about it. How do you tell your parents that the very foundation and bedrock that they taught you has loopholes in it? I can't prove it on paper; however, I feel it in my heart!

I will be the first to admit that I didn't have very many female role models in my life. To be honest, it is one of the things that I longed for as a girl. I didn't have any sisters, cousins, or close aunts to talk with growing up. I had my mom, my grandma, my friends, and societal influences. When I was an adult working my full-time job (in a male-dominated department), I remember thinking to myself, I don't see any women in this organization that I want to model myself after. They are nice people, but I craved role models in my life—someone to look up to, admire, and aspire to be like. When it comes to Christianity, the top two models I think about are Mother Mary and Mary Magdalene. Mother Mary was a virgin. Talk about pressure.

It is hard to open to the possibility that maybe some things your faith taught you are not really the truth. I like to say that my faith held me back and my faith pulled me through. I know I am being led and guided to help other women to be open to the possibility that some of their religious beliefs might be holding them back from the true nature of what God really wants for their lives.

## EXERCISE 1

Our past sexual experiences and desires contribute to shaping our views on sexuality and our bodies and how we feel as women—whether we admit it or not. If we don't address any harbored feelings, talk about them, and release them, they remain dormant inside of us. They stop us from fully experiencing pleasure in our bodies, and they stop us from really becoming the truest versions of ourselves.

Think about your own sexual experiences. You may have never had sex. You may have only been with one person. You may have had a handful of lovers. You may have enjoyed sex and been promiscuous. You may have been raped or inappropriately touched. You may have said "no" but still let it happen anyway. You may have been pregnant and had an abortion. You may have gotten pregnant and had a baby very early in your life. You may have had a miscarriage. You may have had some other experience that has caused you shame around your sexuality or your own pleasure.

All of these experiences impact how you feel about your body and your sexuality. I encourage you to make a list of the "sexual traumas" you may have faced in your life. Go at your own pace. You don't have to tackle this all at once. You do not have to do this alone.

We have been programmed to feel guilty, ashamed, wrong, or bad about our body and our sexual choices. When we acknowledge the feelings, feel them, release them, and take forward the lessons with us, we become free.

**Reflect on the following:**

- When was your first sexual experience?
- Was it a good one?
- Was it consensual or non-consensual?
- Who are the partners you have been with?
- What do you remember about the experience?
- What emotions come to the surface when you think about your past sexual experiences?
- Do guilt or shame creep in and ruin the memories?

## EXERCISE 2

**Take notice of how each statement makes you feel.**

- Self-pleasure or masturbation is wrong.
- Calling your female genitals "pussy" is wrong and disgusting.
- Pleasure is gluttonous and selfish.
- Experiencing pleasure is not important. Your pleasure is not a priority.
- A woman is supposed to satisfy her husband first; it's about his pleasure.
- Sex is for procreation and not pleasure.
- Sex is dirty and messy.
- Sex is only to be experienced during marriage.
- Sex is a sacred act between two people; no toys should be necessary.
- Women who think about sex are provocative and seductive.
- Women who show cleavage are slutty.
- Women who talk about sex are naughty.
- Sex is about making love and not talking dirty. It is meant to be a beautiful, sensual act.
- A classy girl is one who doesn't put on makeup and show off her body.

## EXERCISE 3

**Reflect on what you learned from the church or your spiritual upbringing about sex.**

- Was I taught that sex was for men and that a man's pleasure comes first? Is it my duty as a wife to fulfill my husband's sexual needs?
- Was I taught that sex was just for making babies?
- Was I taught that sex was a healing tool used for purification and pleasure?
- Was I taught that I should only have sex within marriage?
- Was I taught that sex was evil and not something a "good girl" should think about?

## EXERCISE 4

The best lessons we learn in life come from our role models. A role model isn't always necessarily someone who teaches us and tells us what to do, but rather who models for us what is possible through their thoughts, words, values, and actions.

**Journal about the following:**

- Who were the key female role models in your life (mom, grandma, sisters, aunts, coaches, teachers, friend's parents, other)?
- What did the women in your life model for you regarding sex and being a woman?
- What did your mom model for you about sex and being a woman?
- What beliefs or values do you take away from her example and influence?
- What are the things she modeled that you liked?

- What are the things she modeled that you didn't like?
- What feelings show up when you think about what these women taught you about being a woman?
- Did you have someone other than your mom who you could talk to about girly things?

## EXERCISE 5

**Name three different women you admire.**

- Write down five values or characteristics of each woman.
- Circle the overlapping qualities among the women.
- Notice if you would say you have these qualities.

# Notes

# IT'S NOT YOUR FAULT

## TOPIC 1: Sexual Ignorance: You Weren't Taught How to Use a Fork

The first thing that is important to know is, **it is not your fault.** This has been handed down from generation to generation. You wouldn't know any different unless someone taught you differently. Each household teaches a slightly different view on sex and our bodies; however, at the core we have culture, religion, and the media teaching us some of the same basic distorted, unhealthy messages.

This brings me to a story that my dad used to share with me all the time. Whenever I felt like I had failed at something or I felt bad that I didn't do as well as I had expected to, he would ask me, "If you were handed a fork and didn't know how to use it, what would you do? You wouldn't know what to do with it. You could use it to pick a lock on a door. You could use it to undo a tight shoelace. But if no one taught you to eat with a fork, you wouldn't know to use it that way. You would take the fork in your hand and try some things out, but you would never know its real purpose."

You likely wouldn't feel ashamed for not knowing how to use a fork; it was just something no one taught you how to do. It's like if no one ever taught you how to use chopsticks, would you feel bad or shameful that you didn't know how to use them? In our culture today, this is the problem we have with sexuality and our bodies. However, in this instance, we weren't taught about sex and how to love our bodies. Instead, we shame ourselves and others.

*We were* **NOT** *taught how to love, honor, appreciate, respect, and understand our female bodies. We were* **NOT** *taught the beauty of sexuality and the benefits it provides to us.*

## TOPIC 2: Societal Influences: Protection from Risk and Danger

We are in a culture where sex sells. However, if a woman dresses sexy or seductive, she can be labeled as a slut or a whore. I have interviewed many women, and they like feeling sexy; however, many are afraid of what other people might think of them and end up being more reserved. Some of the clients have shared that they are afraid to heal their sexual trauma and their sexuality because they do not want to attract the "wrong kind" of attention.

With the "Me Too" movement, many women are speaking up and sharing their own personal stories. Women are realizing they are not alone in how they feel. They are becoming more comfortable with the idea of healing. They want to explore their sexuality; however, they are afraid of what might happen if they do. They don't want to get hurt again. For some women, it's easier to just keep the door closed than to take a risk and see the beauty that could be on the other side.

No parent wants their daughter to be labeled as a slut or whore at any age. We have been raised culturally to suppress our sexuality because we are afraid. Sex is considered bad, evil, or taboo. If we don't talk about it, then women will be less likely to explore and embrace it.

There are many girls' empowerment movements in which we are looking to teach young girls self-esteem and how to love themselves and their bodies. The intentions are a great start, but there are three important pieces missing.

1. **Recognize the masses do not always do what we say.** It is one thing for an adult to share with a girl the importance of taking care of her body; however, studies show that kids will do what we do, not what we say.

   If you are a mom, a woman of influence, or are in an organization fighting for a better future, and you are telling a young girl to love and protect her body, but you don't love, respect, and take care of your own body, the young girl may not receive the message the way you intended it. We need to lead by example and practice what we preach. The more we can join forces together to make changes within ourselves, we will lead by example and create a ripple effect for future generations.

2. **Understand the generational impact of patriarchal conditioning and power.** We live in a patriarchy where the focus is on the man and power instead of the woman. We don't know any differently because that is what we have been taught for generations. We need to wake up to the fact that we have been conditioned to believe what people want us to believe. It is all about power and control. If you take away the very power source that drives a woman and tell her that it is

shameful and taboo, what a brilliant way to never let her tap into that volcanic source of power. A women's power source lies within her sexuality. If we stifle that and never allow her to unleash the full potential and desires that are inside of her, she will constantly feel a hunger, like something is missing in her life.

3. **Reconnect with and rediscover your body.** How many of us were taught to really take care of and love our bodies? We were taught to clean ourselves and take a shower so we don't smell. We were taught to groom our hair so we don't look like a mop-stick. We were taught to look nice when we go out. We were not taught how to treat our bodies as a temple. We were not taught how to honor, appreciate, and love every part of our bodies. We certainly weren't taught how to enjoy sex.

Our sexuality is at the core of who we are, and, while it might seem taboo, we must talk about it with our younger generations.

According to Peggy Orenstein in a recent TEDx Talk, there was a study done with 300 Dutch and American girls at a university. The Dutch girls had greater self-esteem and embodied everything we say we want for our girls. They had fewer negative consequences like disease, pregnancy, and regret. They experienced more positive outcomes, being able to communicate with their partner, preparing for the experience and responsibility, and enjoying themselves.

What was the difference? The Dutch families had their doctors, teachers, and parents talk candidly, honestly, and openly with them at an early age about sex, pleasure, and the importance of mutual trust.

The American parents weren't necessarily uncomfortable talking about the topic; however, they framed it differently. You see, in the Western world, we teach about the risk and dangers of sex (specifically contraception, disease protection, and, until recently, consent); however, in other cultures they teach the responsibility as well as the joy. There is a big difference when we frame the discussion using the second approach.

> "Sexuality should be a source of self-knowledge, creativity, and communication despite its potential risks. Women should be able to revel in their sexuality without being reduced to it. Women should be able to ask for what they want in bed and get it. They should also feel safe from unwanted pregnancy, disease, cruelty, and violence. We have raised a generation of girls to have a voice to expect egalitarian treatment in the home and the workplace. Is it not time to demand that intimate justice in their personal lives as well?!"
>
> Peggy Orenstein's TED Talk on *What young women believe about their own sexual pleasure.*

This shift can only happen if we normalize the discussions around sex with younger generations and each other.

## TOPIC 3: What God Really Wants for Us

The truth is that God wants us to have a life filled with abundance, fulfillment, pleasure, and prosperity. One of the keys to healing your body and sexual wounds is to challenge your beliefs from the church around sexuality and relationships and truly understand what God wants for us.

Most people have bought into the myth that sex is only to be discussed between a husband and wife, yet while sex is sacred, the topic must be discussed if it's going to be truly honored and protected. We need to educate others on how sexuality is spirituality and if more people understood the depths of this amazing gift, as a society, we would experience less wounding, trauma, and pain in the world. The sad truth is that most people have as much trouble talking about their own funeral as they do talking about sex. It has become uncomfortable to talk about, but it doesn't mean it's not needed. In fact, for men and women to understand the depths and levels of healing, connection, and pleasure, we must talk about it.

In Dr. Gary Smalley's book, *The Language of Sex*, he claims, "God is not afraid of the topic of sex. In fact, God has given us more instructions about sex than He has about parenting. The Bible provides more instruction and guidance for how to make a baby than how to take care of one! God has given us sex as a gift, and it's one to be thoroughly treasured, celebrated, and enjoyed." He goes on to share more about how most sexual issues in marriage can be traced back to relational struggles. The truth is, God designed sex to be so much more than intercourse. When you take an honest look at men and women, and truly understand each other's core needs and desires, you can then find ways to bridge the gap and create the intimacy that you desire.

One of the key principles in the book is the formula to Great Sex: Honor, Security, Intimacy, and Sex. In order to experience great sex, you must first have the three other phases covered. This takes a lot more than just a few minutes of fun in the bedroom. Men and women have different priorities when it comes to intimacy. Men lead with physical intimacy whereas women lead with emotional intimacy. They are both required to help us heal and step into the fullest expression of ourselves.

When you cultivate your relationship and begin to embrace all four stages, you come to know yourself better as a woman and also gain a deeper appreciation for your man. This deep connection based on respect and safety allows you to create the emotional intimacy you crave, which then fuels the physical sex to be amazing. Our relationships can be one of our greatest teachers in life if we allow ourselves to fully embrace all the components of physical and emotional intimacy.

## TOPIC 4: Finding Your Truth: What Is No Longer Serving You?

There are layers of beliefs that have been passed down from generation to generation that are not in alignment with the truth of who we are. It is not about who is right or wrong. It is about what is or is not serving us. It's about being open to the possibility and identifying what beliefs are no longer serving us. What I am saying is that it is each person's responsibility to ***find their own truth***.

We are all called to love and be loved. When we find the truth and love within ourselves, we no longer settle for less than we deserve. When we do that, we also are a living example for others. When we are open to challenging some of the beliefs we have about our body, we can begin the healing process and accept a world of love and beauty that we never knew existed.

Sexual abuse is so rampant these days. According to the National Sex Violence Resource Center, 1 in 5 women have experienced completed or attempted rape in their lifetime, and 81% of women reported experiencing some form of sexual harassment and/or assault in their lifetime. These are only the reported numbers.

We don't have to live with the pain anymore. People who are hurting unwittingly hurt those they love. They don't know any better, and, as a result, they end up settling in unsatisfying and unfulfilling relationships. The behavior typically continues to get handed down to each generation until someone is brave enough to stand up and say enough is enough. We don't need to stay in relationships and tolerate behaviors that are not healthy and fulfilling.

The ironic thing about all of this is that women store emotional pain in our bodies. No wonder we have a hard time liking them. First, we have the societal views around "body image" creating negative self-talk. Then we have the church's views around morality that make us feel bad about our personal, natural desires, and then we have "sexual trauma" all surrounding the body. For each woman, sexual trauma will be different related to her experience. It could be any kind of inappropriate touch or harassment; non-consenting sex; or violent rape and abuse. All these are traumatic in their own way, and the best way to release and heal the pain is through the body itself.

Who wants to love their body when they feel shame, embarrassment, guilt, and all sorts of other feelings around it? But this, in fact, is the answer to our healing. We need to learn how to be with and connect with our body so we can open ourselves up to deeper levels of healing, purification, and eventually pleasure.

There are four categories in which we need healing:

1. Sexual Trauma
2. Societal Influence
3. Church and Generational Beliefs
4. Overall Body Shame

We are carrying all this emotional pain in our body, and no one has taught us how to deal with it and heal the pain. We were taught to settle and deal with the pain rather than release it and heal from it so we can live more fulfilling and happy lives and experience the joy, bliss, pleasure, and ecstasy that God designed for us.

"You are the cause—your beliefs, thoughts, feelings—circumstances are the effect. The sooner you understand, accept, and operate from the notion that you are the source of everything regarding your sexual experiences, the sooner you will heal, recover, and clear space for the deepest, most authentic sexual expression of you. Every woman can experience pleasure and orgasm." —Kim Anami, Sex and Relationship Coach

## TOPIC 5: Witnessing

In my quest for more answers, I looked at what I was taught in my religion around sexuality, and I decided to go straight to the source. I interviewed a priest while I was doing research for this journey, and he said to me, "Jen, sexuality is spirituality." Honestly, I was so relieved to hear these words out of his mouth. I went there for answers, and I certainly got them.

I was intrigued and asked more questions. He said that the way to the spirit was through the body. If you want to have a deeper connection with the Divine, then you need to first connect through your body. If you are not connected to your body, then you will not be able to experience the depth of connection that is available to you. He proceeded to also say that if more people understood this concept, we would have less wounding and trauma in the world and people would be much happier.

I personally struggled with this concept, which is why I feel so strongly about it. I went through tons of pain, questioning, and challenges to come to a point of acceptance.

I did not seek to challenge my roots. I asked God to help me live my calling and my life's purpose. As a result, he continued to show me the way. I like to say that my faith held me back, but my faith pulled me through. I believed in a higher power and continued to use that as my bedrock. I walked blindly in faith, trusting that when I asked, I would receive. There were many times I questioned, "Is this from God or the Devil?" I had to breathe and learn to listen to that small voice inside as opposed to all the voices around me.

One of my biggest passions is that men and women should live healthy, vibrant, loving, intimate relationships. However, before we can truly be intimate with another human being, we must learn to love ourselves and our bodies. There are many books out there that are great at teaching couples how to reconnect and create better marriages. If a couple is meant to be together and can work through their challenges, I am all for that. I also believe that it is each person's choice what they want to experience and have in this lifetime. Do they want to settle for a mediocre relationship, or do they want to create an amazing partnership and friendship of a lifetime?

What I realized on my journey is that I didn't have the best role models when it came to loving my body and having healthy relationships. Many people don't. My parents and grandparents stayed together in unhealthy or less than ideal marriages because they were "supposed to." They settled, believing it was the best for their family. They were not in connection with their bodies and their souls. They were not in tune with the core of who they were. They were afraid to face the truth of their own past and their own hurts. It likely felt safer to be protected and stay in a relationship where they knew what to expect. Yes, they were good, wonderful people. They were religious and believed in God within the limits that were taught to them. They didn't know what they didn't know.

I was mad at my parents and my grandparents for years. I was mad at my grandpa for the abuse in his household. I was mad at my grandma for not doing anything about it. I was mad that this abuse likely happened to other family members and, as a result, my mom didn't know how to protect me from the same type of sexual abuse that occurred. There are hidden secrets in every family that get handed down from generation to generation until someone decides enough is enough!

## *I was the catalyst to say,* "IT STOPS WITH ME!"

I went on a journey to leave behind the things that were no longer serving me. I questioned my Catholic faith and whether it was serving me. I found peace in a different church that felt satisfying to me. Then I left my corporate job; I liked it, but it was not my calling and my passion. I was scared to leave my job, but I knew I needed to in order to do the work I was meant to do in this lifetime. God provided an opportunity for me to leave my job in January 2016. It was divine timing.

Then I left my marriage. I had put forth a ton of effort to make my marriage work. I tried to set expectations about what each of us wanted in a relationship, but it didn't go anywhere. We drifted farther apart. I tried everything, even a 40-day love dare. At the end of the 40 days, we both knew that our lives were not meant to be with each other. Through this whole time, I had been diving into healing deep wounds with my body. I even wrote a letter to my parents sharing my experience of my sexual abuse. It was one of the hardest things I ever did, but I had to do it—not just for my own healing, but for past and future generations.

A few weeks before my divorce, I was at a retreat, and the instructor had us do some visualization exercises. I was shown images of past generations of my family. The message being delivered to me was that they stayed married because of their faith, not because of true love. I energetically told my parents I give them back their Catholic teachings that were no longer serving me. I was standing there next to my new partner and soulmate, stopping this for future generations. I know I will have the intimate connection that I desire with a partner and lover. My best friend.

Right before I got divorced, the judge denied my divorce. I went home and wept. I spent the rest of the weekend in meditation pulling weeds, and it came to me to go back to my roots. Oh my, even though I had recognized the beliefs of the church, somewhere in my subconscious I still believed it was wrong to get divorced. It was like the scarlet letter A. I was tainted and worn. I shouldn't be doing this. So, I took a trip down memory lane and went back to the church where I was raised and asked God to please release me from the shackles that were binding me. To please let this divorce go through and allow both of us to be free to move on with our lives. The fascinating part is that while I let go of this belief, there were still others harboring underneath the covers. Really? Does it go that deep? Yes, unfortunately it does.

### EXERCISE 1

**Reflect on some of the messages in this module.**

Know that it is perfectly okay for you to be feeling triggered; that is part of the process. My faith is my rock, and when I heard messages that contradicted what I had been taught, I struggled with opening to new ideas. I kept praying for God to lead me on the right path, and he kept bringing me back. My faith held me back, but my faith also pulled me through. I was strong enough in my faith to trust a higher power that was leading and guiding me on my soul's path.

- How does the message sit with you?
- What do you feel in your body?
- Are you angry, surprised, shocked, curious, scared, pissed off, triggered?
- What new awareness do you have that feels true for you?
- What statements might be triggering or shocking for you to explore?

## EXERCISE 2

**Listen to "Fear of God."**

- Go to the website and download the song Fear of God. **https://www.thefreedomkeys.com/fear-of-god/**
- Listen to the song.
- Listen again and feel the words.

### Fear of God Song Lyrics

As a little girl I was so afraid
To speak my truth and hear my voice
For the fear of God, I must obey the rules
A good girl, I must be

Good girls get permission, they don't talk back
Apply good judgment, They play it safe
Good girls don't act naughty They work real hard,
They are kind and sweet, and don't complain
So I obeyed the rules, did what I was told
So I would be seen, as that good little girl

Bad girls are lazy, they fool around
They break the rules, and get what they deserve
Bad girls are messy, they get in trouble
they whine and talk back
and turn away from God
For the Fear of God, I must obey the rules
A good little girl, I must be,
So I put up a wall, to protect myself
so I wouldn't get hurt and wouldn't be seen

*Song and Lyrics Written by Jen Bugajsky*

## EXERCISE 3

**Go back through previous exercises and complete two that you skipped.**

## EXERCISE 4

**Review your goals. Did you meet them? Why or why not?**

# Notes

## Did You Enjoy Key #1?

*Are you inspired to continue your healing journey? Here are some great options:*

| The Sensual Feminine Life—What's included | | | |
|---|---|---|---|
| | **OPTION 1 (Good):** | **OPTION 2 (Better):** | **OPTION 3 (Best):** |
| | **Self-Study**—Simply purchase each book in the series separately and work through them at your own pace as a self-study program. | **Group Program**—Join The Sensual Feminine Life Mastery Program where you will receive guidance and inspiration as you become empowered to experience the fullness of the woman you were created to be. | **Private Coaching**—Receive personal coaching and The Sensual Feminine Life Mastery Program to propel you forward more quickly to step into the fullness of the woman you were created to be. |
| All six books (six Keys), including worksheets and integration exercises | ✓ | ✓ | ✓ |
| Twelve months of guidance and support | | ✓ | ✓ |
| Two monthly 90-minute online group coaching calls | | ✓ | ✓ |
| Private Facebook group for community support | | ✓ | ✓ |
| Guided implementation practices and accountability | | ✓ | ✓ |
| Monthly virtual women's circles, rituals, and ceremonies | | ✓ | ✓ |
| Private coaching calls including email and text support | | | ✓ |
| Special bonuses | | | ✓ |

## The Sensual Feminine Life Mastery Program

*A Journey of Self-Discovery to Create Passionate Relationships and a Life You Love*

### No Permission Required

If you desire **to feel sexier, more confident**, and **truly love your body**, mindset alone is not enough. Get out of your head, into your body, and connect with your sensual intelligence and your pleasure. This mastery program is designed to help you reclaim your body, your pleasure, and your power. When you have lost connection with yourself, you can feel numb, disconnected, and unfulfilled. You are here to live the most expressed and embodied version of yourself. This program helps you reclaim the truth of your feminine power and rediscover the joy of being a woman ***so you can joyfully create passionate relationships and a live a life you love!!!***

### The Sensual Feminine Life Mastery Program equips and empowers YOU to enjoy:

- Thriving Relationships—Enjoy deeper closeness, communication, and connection.
- Exquisite Pleasure—Get more, including but not limited to great sex, orgasm, and the simple pleasures of life.
- Sexy Confidence—Feel beautiful, loved, cherished, and desired.

### Discover and unlock the fullest version of YOU with the six keys to freedom:

**Awareness & Discovery**

Gain awareness of historical conditioning around being a woman.

**Permission to Be Curious**

Create focused intention of your needs and desires.

Key Three
the
Goddess

**Acceptance & Personal Responsibility**

Acquire tools to love and appreciate your body.

**Playing with your Feminine Energy**

Learn to explore your body, your energy, and your pleasure.

**Trust, Polarity, & Surrender**

Learn to soften, surrender, and release control.

Key Six
the
Queen

**Worthy & Deserving**

Experience the fulfillment and ecstasy you desire.

## About Jen

Jen inspires and equips women to get out of their heads and into their bodies to embrace more passion and playfulness in their lives. In the past, "girly stuff" was never a top priority for Jen, but as she has embraced her feminine energy, she now deeply understands how important it is for women to feel sexy, confident, and comfortable in their bodies.

Jen uses a combination of mindset tools and body-centered practices (like breath work, pleasure practices, meditation, energy work, sound, and movement) to resolve deep issues holding women back from living their best lives. This multisensory integration of mind and body is the pathway to success.

When a woman feels safe, owns, and truly loves her body and connects with her desires, she will be motivated to heal and live a passionate, playful, and fulfilled life.

## Mission

To empower busy women to rewrite the narrative of their body and reconnect with their femininity and sensuality so they can experience more energy, fulfillment, and pleasure in their business and personal lives in order to be better moms, wives, partners, and friends AND live a lit-up life.

## Vision

I desire to create educational platforms, programs, and experiences that allow a woman to reclaim the wholeness of who she is by embodying her truth despite any fears, connecting with her body and sensuality, and showing up in love and presence so she can share her gifts with the world.

This invitation to womanhood (from a culture that doesn't really understand what this means) creates a sense of warmth, comfort, and safety that allows women to feel safe, knowing they are held in the most loving way, where they dive deeper into themselves in a way they didn't know was possible and couldn't do alone. You can have someone "kick your ass" and push you into action; however, the divine feminine doesn't push, force, or make things happen. She invites you to be on a journey to unlock the doors to your own becoming.

## Impact to the World

- Self-love and self-worth aren't selfish and are a natural expression of being human.
- The body is not viewed as scary, ugly, dirty, or an imperfect disaster waiting to happen.
- Women learn the value of focusing on their own pleasures and desires.
- Better education is provided on love, sex, and relationships.
- Communication on the integration of sexuality and spirituality is more widely explained.
- Healthy sexual activity is not considered taboo, shameful, or dirty.
- Men and women do not suffer in silence with mediocre relationships.

## Contact Jen

Contact Jen at **jen@thefreedomkeys.com**
or reference the following free materials, including:

www.thefreedomkeys.com

www.facebook.com/thefreedomkeys

www.instagram.com/thefreedomkeys/ir

www.linkedin.com/company/the-freedom-keys

www.facebook.com/groups/1020361341358340 (Facebook Group)

The Sensual Feminine Life Podcast starting in fall 2022.

www.ingramcontent.com/pod-product-compliance
Ingram Content Group UK Ltd.
Pitfield, Milton Keynes, MK11 3LW, UK
UKHW062010290726
14090UKWH00022B/1484